THE SE(COPYCAT RECIPES

The cookbook of 35 special dishes to cook at home in a healthy and tasty way from the most famous restaurants in the world . Now here!

Lara Cass

TEST OF CONTENTS

Introduction

Copycat meals or recipes have become very known and popular with the restaurant's ever-high cost of eating.

To begin with, a copycat is an elementary word. It is used to imitate or replicate something done by a person or group of people. It is also used to describe the act of fraud or identification or duplication of someone or something's look. It is also used as the act of imitating or copying something; an exact representation especially in appearance or gesture. The term is also used for something very similar to another.

Most of the time, the word is used when it comes to food. More specifically, desserts. Copycat recipes are top-rated because they are very cheap to make, and the ingredients used are simple and very available. It is also famous as it is the right way of making use of ingredients or food that anyone does not consume. It is also famous for this reason as it helps in recycling the food.

If you have always wanted to cook your favorite restaurant dishes at home without spending a fortune, it's now possible with the help of this cookbook. The recipes are designed to re-create restaurant recipes many people believe would be too complicated to make at home. With easy step-by-step instructions, helpful hints, and easy to follow you can prepare top restaurant dishes in no time.

- 100%-Very Easy Recipes-

- Eliminate expensive and complicated restaurant recipes-

- Tested and approved by home cooks-

- Get the restaurant-quality meal you're craving without the price tag-

- Save time and money-

- Never worry about over-ordering again! -

All dishes are broken down according to course and are carefully written in enough detail to duplicate the pros' exact meal. A rule of thumb, this book has been reported in a more straightforward way. The exciting thing is that the meals in the book are simple, easy to make and inexpensive. They are quick to come off the griddle and grill and require minimal prep work. They have been tested on various men and women, and there is no doubt that they have all enjoyed whatever meal was cooked.

Cooking top secret recipes from restaurants will also make your friends and family wonder where you've learned to cook so well. Imagine cooking a whole meal that looks like it was the restaurant's takeout food. We bet some friends of yours won't even believe you've cooked it! So, hurry! Go to your kitchen and start cooking. Enjoy, and have fun!

Inside you'll find recipes for over seventy popular restaurant meals. Most of them don't take long to prepare and you may already have some of the ingredients in your cupboard. These recipes are delicious. Enjoy!

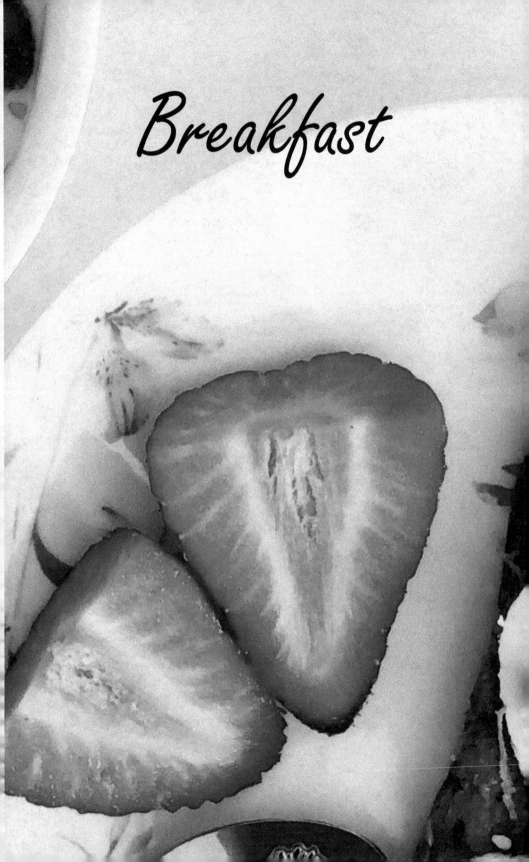

Breakfast

1. French Toast Sticks

Preparation time: 15 minutes

Cooking time: 40 minutes

Servings: 1.5 dozen

Ingredients:

- 6 day-olds Texas toast slices
- 4Large eggs
- 1 cup 2% milk
- .25-.5 tsp Cinnamon
- 2 tbsp Sugar
- 1 tsp Vanilla extract

Optional Ingredients:

- 1 cup Crushed cornflakes
- Confectioner's sugar
- Maple syrup

Directions:

1. Slice each piece of bread into thirds and arrange them in an ungreased pan.

2. Whisk the milk, sugar, eggs, vanilla, and cinnamon. Pour it over the bread and soak for about two minutes, flipping once. Coat the dough with cornflake crumbs.

3. Place in a greased baking pan. Freeze the sticks until firm (45 min.). Store in the freezer.

4. When it's time to eat, add and bake them at 425 °Fahrenheit for eight minutes. Flip them over and cook f until golden brown (10-12 min.).

5. Sprinkle them using the confectioners' sugar and serve with syrup.

Nutrition:

Calories: 380

Carbs: 49g

Fat: 18g

Protein: 5g

2. Ham - Egg & Cheese Biscuit

Preparation time: 15 minutes

Cooking time: 30 minutes

Servings: 10

Ingredients:

- 1 cup Fully cooked ham
- 1 tsp Coarsely ground pepper - divided
- 1 cup Shredded cheddar cheese
- 4 cups Biscuit baking mix
- 1 cup 2% milk
- 3 tbsp Butter

For the Eggs:

- 2 tbsp Butter
- .5 cup 2% milk
- 8 large eggs
- .125 tsp Salt
- .25 tsp Black pepper - coarsely ground
- 1 cup Shredded cheddar cheese

Optional Toppings:

- Sliced tomato

- Red onion

- Salsa

- Avocado

Directions:

1. Chop the ham and green peppers. Warm the oven to reach 425° Fahrenheit.

2. Measure and add the biscuit mix, cheese, ham, and ½ teaspoon of the pepper into a large mixing container. Pour in the milk, stirring until it's just moistened.

3. Scoop it out onto a lightly floured surface, then knead it gently about eight to ten times. Work the dough until it's about a one-inch thickness. Use a floured biscuit cutter to make a 2.5-inch biscuit.

4. Arrange the prepared biscuits about two inches apart on an ungreased baking sheet. Brush with melted butter and dust using the rest of the pepper.

5. Bake the buttered biscuits until golden brown (12-14 min.). Mix the eggs with the milk, pepper, plus salt.

6. Warm a large non-stick skillet using the medium temperature setting to melt the butter.

7. Dump the egg mixture into the pan, stirring until the eggs are thickened and no liquid egg remains. Mix in the cheese and move the pan to a cool burner.

8. Slice the warm biscuits into halves. Layer the bottoms with the egg mixture and toppings as desired. Replace the tops and serve.

Nutrition:

Calories: 370

Carbs: 30g

Fat: 21g

Protein: 16g

Mains

3. Keto Fried Chicken Tenders Chick-Fil-A Copycat Recipe

Preparation time: 10 minutes

Cooking time: 15 minutes

Servings: 8

Ingredients:

- 8 Chicken Tenders
- 24 oz Jar of Dill Pickles juice
- 3/4 Cup Now Foods Almond Flour
- 1 teaspoon salt
- 1 teaspoon Pepper
- 2 Eggs, beaten
- 1 1/2 Cups pork panko
- Nutiva Organic Coconut Oil for frying

Low Carb Copycat Chick-Fil-A Sauce:

- 1/2 Cup Mayo
- 2 tsp Yellow Mustard
- 1 tsp Lemon Juice
- 2 tbs Honey Trees Sugar-Free Honey
- 1 tbs Primal Kitchen Classic BBQ Sauce

Directions:

1. Marinade the chicken tenders in the pickle juice, put it in a large zip lock bag within 1 hour or overnight.

2. Whisk almond flour, salt, plus pepper in a small bowl.

3. Prepare three bowls, the first one with almond flour mixture, then the second bowl is the eggs, and the third bowl is the pork panko.

4. Put the chicken in the almond flour bowl, then in the egg, and finally in the pork panko until well coated.

5. Put 2 inches coconut oil in a pan on medium-high heat.

6. When the oil is hot, put tenders in the oil and cook about 3 minutes on each side or until golden brown.

Low Carb Copycat Chick-Fil-A Sauce:

1. Mix all sauce fixings and stir until thoroughly combined in a small bow.

Nutrition:

Calories: 193.6

Fat: 9 g

Carbs: 1.6 g

Sugar: .5 g

Protein: 26.8 g

4. Chimichicken: Chimichurri Marinated Chicken

Preparation time: 10 minutes

Cooking time: 40 minutes

Servings: 6

Ingredients:

- 6 bone-in, skin-on chicken thighs
- 2 medium sweet potatoes, chopped
- 1 small onion, diced
- 2 tablespoon extra-virgin olive oil

For the marinade:

- 1 bunch fresh flat-leaf parsley
- 1/2 bunch fresh cilantro
- 3 tbsp fresh oregano leaves
- 8 to 10 medium garlic cloves
- 2 teaspoon unrefined salt
- 1/4 cup extra-virgin olive oil
- 1/4 cup red wine vinegar
- juice of 1 lime

Directions:

1. For the marinade, puree all of the fixings in a food processor.

2. Massage each thigh with about 1 tablespoon of the marinade.

3. Marinate in the fridge overnight.

4. Warm the oven at 425F. Put the chopped sweet potatoes plus onion in a single layer on a sheet pan and stir with the 2 tablespoons of EVOO. Sprinkle with salt. Put the thighs on top.

5. Bake within 40-45 minutes. Serve with the remaining EVOO and red wine vinegar.

Nutrition:

Calories: 542

Carbs: 68g

Fat: 15g

Protein: 37g

Sides

5. Café Rio's Fresh Flour Tortillas

Preparation time: 1 hour & 10 minutes

Cooking time: 10 minutes

Servings: 6

Ingredients:

- 3 cups all-purpose flour
- 1 teaspoon salt
- 2 teaspoons baking powder
- ¾ cup lard (or shortening)
- ¾ cup boiling water

Directions:

1. Mix the flour, baking powder, plus salt in a mixing bowl.
2. Cut or rub in the lard (or shortening) until the mixture is evenly crumbly.
3. Put the water and stir until the dough comes together.
4. Turn the dough out onto a lightly floured surface and knead until smooth.
5. Put the dough in a bowl, lightly oiled, covered, then let it sit for one hour.

6. Divide the dough into the number and size of tortillas you want (6 large or 12 small).

7. Heat a skillet or tortilla Comal over medium-high heat. Dampen a clean towel and set out a plate.

8. Form the dough into balls and roll them out thin. You can cut around a plate for a perfect circle.

9. Cook the tortillas for about 1 minute on each side, until the dough is cooked and there are golden spots.

10. Remove the cooked tortilla to the plate and cover it with the towel while you prepare the rest.

Nutrition:

Calories: 180

Carbs: 18g

Fat: 3g

Protein: 3g

6. Chipotle's Cilantro Lime Rice

Preparation time: 5 minutes

Cooking time: 25 minutes

Servings: 6

Ingredients:

- 1 tablespoon vegetable oil
- 1 cup white basmati rice
- 2 tablespoons lime juice
- 1 ½ cups water
- 1 teaspoon salt
- 1 tablespoon fresh cilantro, chopped

Directions:

1. Warm t the oil and add the rice and lime juice in a 2-quart saucepan. Cook and stir for one or two minutes.

2. Add the water and salt. Boil and then lessen the heat and cover.

3. Simmer within 25–30 minutes until the water is absorbed.

4. Fluff it, and stir in the cilantro. Serve.

Nutrition:

Calories: 201

Carbs: 37g

Fat: 3g

Protein: 4g

7. El Torito's Sweet Corn Cake

Preparation time: 10 minutes

Cooking time: 25 minutes

Servings: 6

Ingredients:

- ¼ cup butter
- 2 tablespoons shortening
- ½ cup masa harina
- ¼ cup of cold water
- 10 ounces creamed corn
- 3 tablespoons cornmeal
- ¼ cup of sugar
- 3 tablespoons heavy cream
- ½ teaspoon baking powder
- ¼ teaspoon salt

Directions:

1. Preheat the oven to 350°F. Butter an 8-inch pan (round or square) that will fit inside a roasting pan.

2. Mix the butter plus the shortening until they are fluffy in a mixing bowl.

3. Gradually incorporate the masa harina, and then the water. Mix in the corn.

4. Mix the cornmeal, sugar, heavy cream, baking powder, and salt in a separate bowl.

5. Add the corn mixture to the other ingredients and mix just to combine.

6. Spread the batter in the prepared dish.

7. Place it in the roasting pan, then pour hot water in until it's about an inch deep.

8. Bake within 45–50 minutes until a toothpick inserted in the center comes out clean.

Nutrition:

Calories: 100

Carbs: 22g

Fat: 1g

Protein: 1g

8. Acapulco's Mexican Rice

Preparation time: 10 minutes

Cooking time: 55 minutes

Servings: 6

Ingredients:

- 3 tablespoons lard or chicken fat
- 1 large onion, diced
- 2 cups long-grain rice
- 2 cups chicken broth
- 1 cup tomato juice
- 1 cup diced tomatoes
- 1 tablespoon chopped parsley
- 2 cloves garlic, minced
- ½ teaspoon paprika
- ½ teaspoon ground cumin
- 1 teaspoon salt
- 1 dash white pepper

Directions:

1. Warm the oven to 350°F and butter a casserole dish.

2. In a skillet, melt the lard or chicken fat. Cook the onion and rice until they are lightly browned, about 10 minutes, stirring constantly. Transfer them to the prepared dish.

3. In the skillet, combine the remaining ingredients and bring them to a boil. Pour them over the rice and mix.

4. Covered it with foil and baked within 25–30 minutes. Fluff with a fork, and serve.

Nutrition:

Calories: 199

Carbs: 29g

Fat: 8g

Protein: 3g

9. Chili's Black Bean

Preparation time: 5 minutes

Cooking time: 25 minutes

Servings: 6

Ingredients:

- 2 cans (15.5-ounces each) black beans
- ½ teaspoon sugar
- 1 teaspoon ground cumin
- 1 teaspoon chili powder
- ½ teaspoon garlic powder
- 2 tablespoon red onion, diced finely
- ½ teaspoon fresh cilantro, minced (optional)
- ½ cup of water
- Salt and black pepper to taste
- Pico de Gallo and or sour cream for garnish (optional)

Directions:

1. Combine the beans, sugar, cumin, chili powder, garlic, onion, cilantro (if using), and water in a saucepan and mix well.

2. Over medium-low heat, let the bean mixture simmer for about 20-25 minutes—season with salt and pepper to taste.

3. Remove the beans from heat and transfer to serving bowls.

4. Garnish with Pico de Gallo or a dollop of sour cream, if desired.

Nutrition:

Calories: 320

Carbs: 53g

Fat: 8g

Protein: 14g

Seafood

10. Tony Roma's Grilled Salmon with Carolina Honeys Sauce

Preparation time: 5 minutes

Cooking time: 60 minutes

Servings: 4

Ingredients:

- 1 cup ketchup
- 1 cup apple cider vinegar
- ½ cup molasses
- ½ cup honey
- 1 teaspoon hickory liquid smoke
- 1½ teaspoons salt, divided
- ½ teaspoon garlic powder, divided
- ¼ teaspoon onion powder
- ¼ teaspoon Tabasco pepper sauce
- ½ teaspoon ground black pepper
- ¼ teaspoon paprika
- ¼ teaspoon ground cayenne pepper
- 4 6-ounce skinless salmon fillets
- Olive oil cooking spray or olive oil

Directions:

1. To make the sauce, add ketchup, vinegar, molasses, honey, liquid smoke, ½ teaspoon salt, ¼ teaspoon garlic powder, onion powder, and Tabasco sauce to a deep pan.

2. Heat over medium-high heat, stirring to mix until smooth. Bring to a boil, then reduce heat. Let simmer within 30 minutes until the mixture becomes thick.

3. Spray or brush grill with olive oil. Preheat grill to high heat.

4. Prepare dry seasoning by mixing remaining salt and garlic powder, black pepper, paprika, and cayenne pepper in a bowl.

5. Rub salmon with seasoning mixture on all sides. Add salmon to grill and cook for 3 minutes. Rotate to 180 degrees to create crisscross marks, then turn.

6. Repeat process with the other side. Remove from grill once fillets are cooked through.

7. Transfer to a serving plate. Serve with sauce drizzled on top.

Nutrition:

calories 579

fat 10 g

carbs 86 g

sugar 58 g

fibers 0 g

protein 36 g

11. Red Lobster's Cajun Shrimp

Preparation time: 10 minutes

Cooking time: 15 minutes

Servings: 4

Ingredients:

- ½ cup butter, melted
- 1-pound medium shrimp, peeled and deveined
- 4 teaspoons cayenne pepper
- 3 teaspoons salt
- 2 teaspoons black pepper
- 2 teaspoons paprika
- 2 teaspoons cumin
- 2¼ teaspoons dry mustard
- 1 teaspoon dried thyme
- 1 teaspoon dried oregano
- 2 teaspoons onion powder
- 2 teaspoons garlic powder
- Lemon wedges

Directions:

1. Preheat oven to 400°F.

2. Coat the bottom of a baking tray using a butter. Arrange shrimp onto the tray.

3. Combine remaining ingredients in a bowl and rub onto shrimp to season. Make sure shrimp are thoroughly and evenly coated with both butter and seasoning mixture.

4. Place in oven and bake for about 10 to 15 minutes until color changes.

5. Serve with lemon wedges on the side.

Nutrition:

Calories 341

Fat 25 g

Carbs 5 g

Sugar 1 g

Fibers 2 g

Protein 25 g

12. Applebee's" Honey Grilled Salmon

Preparation time: 15 minutes

Cooking time: 23 minutes

Servings: 4

Ingredients:

- 4 teaspoons olive oil, divided
- ¼ cup dark brown sugar, packed
- ¼ cup pineapple juice
- 2 tablespoons fresh lemon juice
- 2 tablespoons white distilled vinegar
- ½ teaspoon paprika
- ½ teaspoon cayenne pepper
- ¼ teaspoon garlic powder
- Salt and ground black pepper, as required
- 4 salmon fillets

Directions:

1. In a saucepan, add 2 teaspoons of oil and remaining ingredients except for salmon fillets over medium-low heat and boil, stirring occasionally.

2. Adjust to low, then simmer, uncovered for about 15 minutes, stirring occasionally.

3. Preheat the barbecue grill to medium heat. Grease the grill grate. Rub the salmon fillets with remaining olive oil and sprinkle with salt and pepper.

4. Place the salmon fillets onto the grill and cook for about 3-4 minutes per side.

5. Remove the salmon fillets from the grill and brush each fillet with the honey sauce. Serve hot.

Nutrition:

Calories: 276

Fat: 13.6g

 Protein: 27.7g

Carbs: 11.5g

Fiber: 0.2g

Sugar: 10.6g

13. Long Johns Silver's" Batter-Dipped Fish

Preparation time: 15 minutes

Cooking time: 6 minutes

Servings: 6

Ingredients:

- 2 cups flour
- ¼ cup cornstarch
- 2 teaspoons sugar
- ½ teaspoon baking soda
- ½ teaspoon baking powder
- ½ teaspoon paprika
- ½ teaspoon onion salt
- Salt and ground black pepper, as required
- 16 ounces club soda
- 2 pounds cod, cut into 3-ounce slices
- 2-3 cups vegetable oil

Directions:

1. In a large bowl, add flour, cornstarch, sugar, baking soda, baking powder, paprika, onion salt, salt, and black pepper and mix well.

2. Put the club soda and mix until well combined. Coat the fish slices with flour mixture evenly.

3. Warm-up the oil in a large skillet and fry the fish slices for about 2-3 minutes or until golden brown.

4. Transfer the fish slices onto a paper towel-lined plate to drain. Serve warm.

Nutrition:

Calories: 942

Fat: 74.5g

Protein: 38.9g

Carbs: 38.3g

Fiber: 1.3g

Sugar: 1.5g

14. Popeye's" Cajun Fish

Preparation time: 15 minutes

Cooking time: 8 minutes

Servings: 4

Ingredients:

- 2 pounds boneless, skinless catfish fillets, cut into 2-inch strips
- 1 cup buttermilk
- 1 large egg
- ¼ cup flour
- ¼ cup corn muffin mix
- 1 teaspoon Louisiana hot sauce
- 1 teaspoon dried oregano
- 1 teaspoon dried thyme
- 2 teaspoons ground mustard
- 2½ teaspoons paprika
- 2 teaspoons garlic powder
- 1 teaspoon onion powder
- 1 teaspoon cayenne pepper
- 2 teaspoons ground black pepper
- Salt, as required

- ½ cup of vegetable oil

Directions:

1. In a large bowl, soak the fish strips in buttermilk for about 30-45 minutes.

2. In a separate bowl, add egg, flour, and corn mix and beat until smooth.

3. Add the hot sauce, herbs, mustard, and spices and stir to combine.

4. Refrigerate the mixture for about 10-15 minutes.

5. Remove the fish strips from buttermilk and then coat with flour mixture evenly.

6. Warm-up the oil over medium-high heat in a large skillet and fry fish strips for about 3-4 minutes per side.

7. With a slotted spoon, transfer the fish strips onto a paper towel-lined plate to drain. Serve warm.

Nutrition:

Calories: 692

Fat: 48.8g

Protein: 41.9g

Carbs: 22.2g

Fiber: 3.5g

Sugar: 6.1g

15. Bonefish Grill" Pan-Fried Tilapia with Chimichurri Sauce

Preparation time: 15 minutes

Cooking time: 8 minutes

Servings: 4

Ingredients:

For Tilapia:

- 4 tilapia fillets
- 2 tablespoons BBQ seasoning
- Salt and ground black pepper, as required
- 2 teaspoons olive oil

For Chimichurri Sauce:

- 8 garlic cloves, minced
- Salt, as required
- 1 teaspoon dried oregano
- 1 teaspoon ground black pepper
- 1 teaspoon red pepper flakes, crushed
- 4-5 teaspoons lemon zest, grated finely
- 4 ounces fresh lemon juice

- 1 bunch fresh flat-leaf parsley
- 1 cup olive oil

Directions:

1. For Chimichurri sauce: in a food processor, add all ingredients and pulse until well combined.

2. Transfer the sauce into a bowl and refrigerate to marinate for 30 minutes before serving.

3. Meanwhile, for tilapia: season each tilapia fillet with BBQ seasoning, salt, and black pepper.

4. Warm-up oil over medium-high heat in a non-stick pan and cook the tilapia fillets for about 3-4 minutes on each side.

5. Divide tilapia fillets onto serving plates.

6. Top each fillet with Chimichurri sauce and serve.

Nutrition:

Calories: 570

Fat: 52.1g

Protein: 27.2g

Carbs: 3.9g

Fiber: 0.8g

Sugar: 0.9g

Poultry

16. Cracker Barrel's Campfire Chicken

Preparation Time: 10 minutes

Cooking Time: 45 minutes

Servings: 4

Ingredients:

- 1 tablespoon paprika
- 2 teaspoons onion powder
- 2 teaspoons salt
- 1 teaspoon garlic powder
- 1 teaspoon dried rosemary
- 1 teaspoon black pepper
- 1 teaspoon dried oregano
- 1 whole chicken, quartered
- 2 carrots, cut into thirds
- 3 red skin potatoes, halved
- 1 ear of corn, quartered
- 1 tablespoon olive oil
- 1 tablespoon butter
- 5 sprigs fresh thyme

Directions:

1. Preheat the oven to 400°F.

2. Mix the paprika, onion powder, salt, garlic powder, rosemary, pepper, and oregano.

3. Add the chicken quarters and 1 tablespoon of the spice mix to a large plastic freezer bag. Cover and put inside the refrigerator for at least 1 hour.

4. Put the carrots, corn, and potatoes in a bowl. Put some olive oil and the rest of the spice mix. Toss to coat.

5. Preheat a large skillet over high heat. Add some oil, and when it is hot, add the chicken pieces and cook until golden brown.

6. Prepare 4 pieces of aluminum foil and add some carrots, potatoes, corn, and a chicken quarter to each. Top with some butter and thyme.

7. Fold the foil in and make pouches by sealing the edges tightly—Bake for 45 minutes.

Nutrition:

Calories: 140

Fat: 8g

Carbs: 30

Sugars: 10g

Protein: 25g

17. Cracker Barrel's Chicken and Dumplings

Preparation Time: 30 minutes

Cooking Time: 20 minutes

Servings: 4

Ingredients:

- 2 cups flour
- ½ teaspoon baking powder
- 1 pinch salt
- 2 tablespoons butter
- 1 scant cup buttermilk
- 2 quarts chicken broth
- 3 cups cooked chicken

Directions:

1. Mix in a bowl the salt, flour, and baking powder in a large bowl to make the dumplings. Cut the butter into the flour mixture. Put in the milk until it forms a dough ball.

2. Put enough flour on your working station. Roll out your dough relatively thin, then cut into squares to form dumplings.

3. Flour a plate and transfer the dough from the counter to the plate.

4. Bring the chicken broth to a boil in a large saucepan, then drop the dumplings in one by one, stirring continually.

5. The excess flour will thicken the broth. Cook it for 20-25 minutes or until the dumplings are no longer doughy.

6. Add the chicken, stir to combine, and serve.

Nutrition:

Calories: 115

Fat: 14g

Carbs: 78g

Sugars: 9g

Protein: 8g

18. Red Lobster's Classic BBQ Chicken

Preparation time: 5 minutes

Cooking time: 1 hour 45 minutes

Servings: 4–6

Ingredients:

- 4 pounds of chicken
- Salt
- Olive oil
- 1 cup barbecue sauce

Directions:

1. Put some olive oil and salt all over the chicken. In the meanwhile, preheat the griddle with high heat.

2. Grill the chicken skin side for 10 minutes. Cover the chicken with foil and grill for 30 minutes in low heat.

3. Put some barbecue sauce all over the chicken. Cook the chicken for another 20 minutes.

4. Baste, cover, and cook again for 30 minutes.

5. Baste with more barbecue sauce to serve!

Nutrition:

Calories: 539

Fat: 11.6g

Carbs: 15.1g

Sugar: 0.3g

Protein: 87.6g

19. Chipotle's Grilled Sweet Chili Lime Chicken

Preparation time: 35 minutes

Cooking time: 15 minutes

Servings: 4

Ingredients:

- ½ cup sweet chili sauce
- ¼ cup of soy sauce
- 1 teaspoon marina juice
- 1 teaspoon orange juice, fresh squeezed
- 1 teaspoon orange marmalade
- 2 tablespoons lime juice
- 1 tablespoon brown sugar
- 1 clove garlic, minced
- 4 boneless, skinless chicken breasts
- Sesame seeds, for garnish

Directions:

1. Whisk sweet chili sauce, soy sauce, marina, orange marmalade, lime and orange juice, brown sugar, and the minced garlic together in a small mixing bowl.

2. Set aside ¼ cup of the sauce. Coat the chicken in sauce to coat and let it marinate 30 minutes.

3. Preheat your griddle to medium heat. Cook each side of the chicken on the grill for 7 minutes.

4. Baste the cooked chicken with remaining marinade and garnish with sesame seeds to serve with your favorite sides.

Nutrition:

Calories: 380

Sugar: 0.5g

Fat: 12g

Carbs: 19.7g

Protein: 43.8g

20. Chipotle's Adobo Chicken

Preparation time: 1 –24 hours

Cooking time: 20 minutes

Servings: 4 – 6

Ingredients:

- 2 lbs. chicken thighs or breasts (boneless, skinless)

For the marinade:

- ¼ cup olive oil
- 2 chipotle peppers
- 1 teaspoon adobo sauce
- 1 tablespoon garlic, minced
- 1 shallot, finely chopped
- 1 ½ tablespoons cumin
- 1 tablespoon cilantro, super-finely chopped or dried
- 2 teaspoons chili powder
- 1 teaspoon dried oregano
- ½ teaspoon salt
- Fresh limes, garnish
- Cilantro, garnish

Directions:

1. Preheat grill to medium-high. Blend the marinade ingredients to turn it into a paste.

2. Add the chicken and marinade to a sealable plastic bag and massage to coat well.

3. Put in the fridge before grilling. Grill the chicken for 7 minutes, turn and grill an additional 7 minutes; or until good grill marks appear.

4. Continue to grill in low heat until chicken is cooked through, and the internal temperature reaches 165°F.

5. After that, remove it from the grill and allow to rest 5 to 10 minutes before serving.

6. Squeeze fresh lime and sprinkle cilantro to serve.

Nutrition:

Calories: 561

Sugar: 0.3g

Fat: 23.8g

Carbs: 18.7g

21. Chipotle's Classic Grilled Chicken

Preparation time: 8 – 24 hours

Cooking time: 20 minutes

Servings: 4

Ingredients:

- 2 lbs. boneless, skinless chicken thighs

For the marinade:

- ¼ cup fresh lime juice
- 2 teaspoon lime zest
- ¼ cup honey
- 2 tablespoons olive oil
- 1 tablespoon balsamic vinegar
- ½ teaspoon of sea salt
- ½ teaspoon black pepper
- 2 garlic cloves, minced
- ¼ teaspoon onion powder

Directions:

1. Mix the marinade fixings in a large bowl; reserve 2 tablespoons of the marinade for grilling.

2. Add chicken and marinade to a sealable plastic bag and marinate 8 hours or overnight in the refrigerator.

3. Preheat grill to medium heat and brush lightly with olive oil. Put the chicken on the grill and cook 8 minutes per side.

4. Coat the chicken in the marinade in the last few minutes of cooking until it reaches the internal temperature of 165°F.

5. Place the chicken, tent with foil, and allow resting for 5 minutes. Serve and enjoy!

Nutrition:

Calories: 381

Sugar: 1.1g

Fat: 20.2g

Carbs: 4.7g

Protein: 44.7g

Meat

22. Meat Loaf

Preparation Time: 15 minutes

Cooking Time: 1 ½ hour

Servings: 6

Ingredients:

- 2 large eggs
- 2/3 cup whole milk
- 3 slices bread, torn
- 1/2 cup chopped onion
- 1/2 cup grated carrot
- 1 cup shredded cheddar
- 1 tablespoon parsley, minced
- 1 teaspoon dried basil
- 1 teaspoon salt
- 1/4 teaspoon pepper
- 1-1/2 pounds lean ground beef

Topping:

- 1/2 cup tomato sauce
- 1/2 cup packed brown sugar
- teaspoon prepared mustard

Directions:

1. Whisk the eggs in a bowl, then put the milk plus bread. Mix in the onion, carrot, cheese, plus the seasonings.

2. Put the beef over mixture, then shape into a 7-1/2x3-1/2x2-1/2 inches loaf in a shallow baking pan. Bake it uncovered, at 350° within 45 minutes.

3. Mix the topping fixings, spoon half of the batter over the meatloaf.

4. Bake within 30 minutes. Allow to cool down within 10 minutes before serving.

Nutrition:

Calories: 200

Carbs: 11g

Fat: 11g

Protein: 18g

23. Roast Beef

Preparation Time: 20 minutes

Cooking Time: 2 ½ hours

Servings: 8

Ingredients:

- 1 tbsp canola oil
- 1 beef eye round roast
- 1 garlic clove, minced
- 2 tsp dried basil
- 1 tsp salt
- 1 tsp dried rosemary, crushed
- 1/2 tsp pepper
- 1 medium onion, chopped
- 1 teaspoon beef bouillon granules
- 1 cup brewed coffee
- 3/4 cup water

Gravy:

- 1/4 cup all-purpose flour
- 1/4 cup cold water

Directions:

1. Warm oil over medium heat in a Dutch oven; brown roast over all sides. Remove, then mix garlic plus seasonings, and sprinkle on the roast.

2. Put the onion into the same pan; cook on medium heat. Mix in the bouillon, coffee plus 3/4 cup water, then put the roast and boil.

3. Simmer, covered, within 2-1/2 hours, remove roast from pan, and set aside cooking juices. Cover it with foil, then let it cool down within 10 minutes.

4. Mix the flour plus cold water, then stir into cooking juices. Boil while stirring continuously—Cook and stir until thickened, 1-2 minutes. Serve with roast.

Nutrition:

Calories: 198

Fat: 6g

Cholesterol: 65mg

Sodium: 453mg

Carbohydrate: 5g

Protein: 28g

24. Grilled Pork Chops

Preparation Time: 20 minutes

Cooking Time: 10 minutes

Servings: 4

Ingredients:

- 1/4 cup kosher salt
- 1/4 cup sugar
- 2 cups of water
- 2 cups of ice water
- 4 center-cut pork rib chops
- 2 tablespoons canola oil

Basic Rub:

- 3 tablespoons paprika
- 1 teaspoon each:
- garlic powder
- onion powder
- ground cumin
- ground mustard
- 1 teaspoon coarsely ground pepper
- 1/2 teaspoon ground chipotle pepper

Directions:

1. Mix the salt, sugar, and 2 cups water in a large saucepan; cook on medium heat, then remove.

2. Put 2 cups ice water to cool brine at room temperature. Put the pork chops in a large Ziplock bag; put the cooled brine, seal, and coat the chops.

3. Put it in a 13x9-in. Baking dish then cools it in the fridge within 8-12 hours. Pat-dry the chops from the brine, then discard the brine. Drizzle both sides of chops using oil.

4. Mix the rub fixings in a small bowl, then rub it onto pork chops. Let stand at room temperature 30 minutes.

5. Grill chops on an oiled rack, covered, over medium heat 4-6 minutes on each side or until a thermometer read 145°. Let stand 5 minutes before serving.

Nutrition:

Calories: 300

Fat: 18g

Cholesterol: 72mg

Sodium: 130mg

Carbohydrate: 5g

Protein: 30g

25. Peppered Ribeye Steaks

Preparation Time: 10 minutes

Cooking Time: 10 minutes

Servings: 8

Ingredients:

- 1 tbsp garlic powder
- 1 tbsp paprika
- 2 tsp dried ground thyme
- 2 tsp dried ground oregano
- 1-1/2 tsp kosher salt
- 1-1/2 tsp pepper
- 1 tsp lemon-pepper seasoning
- 1 tsp cayenne pepper
- 1 tsp crushed red pepper flakes
- 4 beef ribeye steaks

Directions:

1. Mix all the seasonings, then sprinkle it over the steaks.

2. Marinate it in the fridge within 1 hour or up to 24 hours. Remove and pat dry with paper towels, but leave the garlic mixture on steaks as possible.

3. Grill the steaks, covered, turning occasionally.

4. Move the steaks to direct heat; continue to grill until meat reaches desired doneness.

5. Let it cool down within 5 minutes before slicing and serve.

Nutrition:

Calories: 257

Fat: 18g

Cholesterol: 67mg

Sodium: 453mg

Carbohydrate: 2g

Protein: 21g

26. Mushroom Braised Pot Roast

Preparation Time: 10 minutes

Cooking Time: 1 hour 30 minutes

Servings: 10

Ingredients:

- 4 pounds chuck roast
- 2 tablespoons vegetable oil
- 1/2 teaspoon salt
- 1/4 teaspoon pepper
- 1 cup chopped onion
- 2 cups beef broth
- 2 tablespoons gravy master
- 2 tablespoons butter
- 1-pound cremini mushrooms sliced or white button mushrooms
- 1/2 teaspoon salt

Directions:

1. Rub the roast with salt plus pepper, then put the vegetable oil in the Instant Pot and brown the roast all over.

2. Put 1 chopped onion with 2 cups of beef broth and 2 tablespoons of Gravy Master. Use the meat-setting button within 90 minutes.

3. Let the pot to release by using the natural release method.

4. While the pot is releasing the pressure, naturally sauté 1 pound of sliced mushrooms butter.

5. Put 1/2 teaspoon of salt to the mushrooms while sautéing.

6. When mushrooms are cooked through, add to the roast.

Nutrition:

Calories: 392

Carbohydrates: 3g

Protein: 37g

Fat: 26g

Cholesterol: 131mg

Sodium: 782mg

Potassium: 862mg

Sugar: 1g

Vegetables

27. Eggplant Parmigiana

Preparation time: 2 hours

Cooking time: 30 minutes

Servings: 3

Ingredients:

- 1 large eggplant
- Flour (for dusting)
- 1 egg
- ½ pound mozzarella cheese, shredded
- 1¾ cups milk
- 1 tablespoon clarified butter
- 2 teaspoons olive oil
- 1 (24-ounce) jar marinara sauce
- 1 cup dry breadcrumbs
- ¾ cup parmesan cheese
- Salt and pepper, to taste

Directions:

1. Preheat oven to 350°F.

2. Prepare eggplant by blanching and peeling. Cut into ½-inch-thick slices. Put in a colander, then sprinkle with salt. Let drain for 30 minutes. Rinse and dry. Set aside.

3. Place egg, milk, and olive oil in a mixing bowl. In a separate bowl, mix breadcrumbs and parmesan, then in a third bowl, place flour.

4. Dip eggplant slices into the flour. Remove the excess, then dip into the egg wash. Let excess drip off, then toss into bread crumbs to coat thoroughly. Set aside to dry for about 1 hour.

5. Grease a baking pan with olive oil. Melt butter in a sauté pan and sauté the eggplant slices until golden on both sides. Transfer to the greased baking pan.

6. Cover the slices in mozzarella cheese and pour tomato sauce on top—Bake for 10 minutes. Let cool.

7. Sprinkle with oregano. Best served with pasta.

Nutrition:

Calories: 270

Carbs: 26g

Fat: 15g Protein: 8g

28. Gnocchi with Spicy Tomato and Wine Sauce

Preparation time: 10 minutes

Cooking time: 40 minutes

Servings: 4

Ingredients:

Sauce:

- 2 tablespoons extra virgin olive oil
- 6 fresh garlic cloves
- ½ teaspoon chili flakes
- 1 cup dry white wine
- 1 cup chicken broth
- 2 cans (14.5 ounces each) tomatoes
- ¼ cup fresh basil, chopped
- ¼ cup sweet, creamy butter, cut into 1-inch cubes, chilled
- ½ cup parmesan cheese, freshly grated

Pasta:

- 1-pound gnocchi
- Salt, to taste

- Black pepper, freshly crushed, to taste

Directions:

1. Put the olive oil, garlic, plus chili flakes in a cold pan and cook over medium heat.

2. Put the wine and broth and bring the mixture to a simmer.

3. After about 10 minutes, the broth should be halved. When that happens, add in the tomatoes and basil and then let the sauce continue simmering for another 30 minutes.

4. Set aside the sauce once it thickens to cool for 3 minutes.

5. After 3 minutes, place the sauce in a blender, and add the butter and parmesan. Purée everything together and set aside.

6. Prepare the pasta by boiling the gnocchi in a large pot. When it is cooked, strain the pasta and mix with the sauce.

7. Transfer everything to a plate and serve.

Nutrition:

Calories: 266

Carbs: 33g

Fat: 0g

Protein: 10g

Soups & Stews

29. Carrabba's Mama Mandola Sicilian Chicken Soup

Preparation Time: 15 minutes

Cooking Time: 8 hours

Servings: 10

Ingredients:

- 4 carrots, peeled, diced
- 4 stalks celery, diced
- 1 green bell pepper, cored, diced
- 2 medium white potatoes, diced
- 1 white onion, diced
- 3 cloves garlic, minced
- 1 can (14.5 ounces) tomatoes, diced, with juice
- 1 tablespoon fresh parsley
- 1 teaspoon Italian seasoning
- ½ teaspoon white pepper
- crushed red pepper flakes
- 2 boneless skinless chicken breasts, shredded
- 32-ounces containers chicken stock
- 1 ½ teaspoons salt
- 1-pound Ditalini pasta

Directions:

1. Dice and chop the vegetables as instructed.

2. Place them in a slow cooker and sprinkle with the parsley, seasoning, and white and red pepper. Mix everything.

3. Add the shredded chicken and stock and remix it.

4. Cover the mixture and cook it for 8 hours on low heat.

5. When the soup is nearly cooked, bring a salt-and-water mixture to a boil to cook the pasta.

6. Add the cooked pasta to the soup. Cook for another 5 minutes and serve.

Nutrition:

Calories: 320

Fat: 0 g

Protein: 13 g

Carbs: 57 g

30. Carrabba's Sausage and Lentil Soup

Preparation Time: 10 minutes

Cooking Time: 1 hour 5 minutes

Servings: 6

Ingredients:

- 1-pound Italian sausages
- 1 large onion, diced
- 1 stalk celery, diced
- 2 large carrots, diced
- 1 small zucchini, diced
- 6 cups low sodium chicken broth
- 2 cans (14.5 ounces each) tomatoes, chopped, with juice
- 2 cups dry lentils
- 2–3 garlic cloves, minced
- 1 ½ teaspoons salt
- 1 teaspoon black pepper
- 1-3 pinches red pepper flakes
- 1 teaspoon dry basil
- ½ teaspoon dry oregano
- ½ teaspoon parsley

- ½ teaspoon dry thyme

- Parmesan cheese for garnishing

Directions:

1. Preheat the oven to 350°F. Place sausages on a baking dish and poke a few holes in each link with a fork. Bake until the sausages are finished (around 20-30 minutes)

2. Let the sausages cool down and slice.

3. Chop and thin the ingredients as set out in the list of ingredients.

4. Put all the fixings in a large pot, except for the Parmesan cheese.

5. Let the mixture simmer for an hour, adding water where necessary to reduce thickness. Puree a portion of the soup, and return it if you want a thicker soup.

6. Before serving, ladle the soup in bowls and garnish with parmesan cheese.

Nutrition:

Calories: 221

Fat: 10 g

Protein: 13 g

Carbs: 20 g

Snacks

31. Taco Bell Chicken Burrito

Preparation Time: 25–30 minutes

Cooking Time: 35 minutes

Servings: 3

Ingredients:

- 1 lb. of boneless skinless chicken breasts
- 2 (8 ounces) cans of tomato sauce
- 1 tablespoon of olive oil
- 2 teaspoons of white vinegar
- 3 garlic cloves (minced)
- ½ teaspoon of sugar
- 1 teaspoon of ground cumin
- 2 teaspoons of oregano
- Salt and pepper (to taste)
- 4 teaspoons of chili powder
- Lime and Cilantro Rice
- ½ tablespoon of butter
- 2 cups of chicken broth
- ¼ teaspoon of cumin
- 1 cup of long-grain white rice

- ¾ teaspoon of salt

- ¼ teaspoon of ground black pepper

- 2 tablespoons of chopped cilantro

- Juice and zest of 1 lime

Avocado-Ranch Dressing:

- ½ avocado

- ¼ cup of ranch dressing

- 1/8 cup of buttermilk

- 2 tablespoons of sour cream

- 1 teaspoon of salt

For assembly:

- 6 pieces of flour tortillas

- 2 cups of shredded cheddar cheese

Directions:

1. Combine ranch dressing, avocado, buttermilk, sour cream, and salt in a blender and pulse until it becomes smooth. Chill while not in use.

2. In a large pan, heat oil and put in chicken breasts, add tomato sauce and simmer until the chicken is cooked thoroughly.

3. Transfer it to a flat dish and shred. Put it back to the sauce and continue simmering until the most liquid's absorbed.

4. Then, start making the lime-cilantro rice by melting butter in a saucepan. Put in your rice grains and coat with butter.

5. Add chicken broth, lime juice, zest, pepper, salt, and cumin. Boil and lower down to a simmering heat. Cook until the rice is tender.

6. Wrap the tortilla in a damp towel and heat in the microwave for 3–5 minutes.

7. Lay the tortilla on a plate, add dressing, chicken rice, and lastly, top with shredded cheese. Fold, serve, and enjoy.

Nutrition:

Calories: 350

Fat: 10g

Carbs: 47g

Protein: 19g

32. Taco Bell Cheese Potato Burrito

Preparation Time: 15-25 minutes

Cooking Time: 25 -30 minutes

Servings: 4

Ingredients:

Homemade taco seasoning:

- 2 tablespoon of corn starch
- 2 tablespoons of all-purpose flour
- 3 1/2 teaspoons of granulated beef bouillon
- 1 teaspoon of garlic powder
- 1 1/2 teaspoon of paprika
- 1 teaspoon of granulated sugar
- 1 teaspoon of chili powder
- 1 teaspoon of cumin
- 1 teaspoon of onion powder
- ¼ teaspoon of natural unsweetened cocoa powder

For ground beef:

- ½ lb. of ground beef

- 2/3 cup of water

Potato filling:

- Oil for frying

- 3/4-pound of potatoes (about 2 medium), peeled and cut into 1/2-in. cubes

Assembly:

- 8 flour tortillas (10 inches), warmed

- 4 cups of shredded Mexican cheese blend

Directions:

1. Taco Seasoning: Add all the ingredients under the homemade taco seasoning in a bowl and mix until well combined.

2. Ground beef Tacos: Heat oil in a pan and sauté and brown ground beef. Remove excess fat.

3. Add water to the pan and the taco seasoning you just made. Bring to a boil, then lower down to a simmering heat.

4. Cook within 15 minutes, stirring constantly. At the same time, reheat fried beans to low heat in a pan.

5. For the Potato filling, heat oil to 200°C, then fry potatoes per batch until crispy outside and tender inside.

6. Assembly: Lay tortilla on a warm pan and heat both sides; add ground meat, shredded Mexican cheese, and potatoes. And fold the tortilla. Serve and enjoy.

Nutrition:

Calories: 480

Fat: 22g

Carbs: 55g

Protein: 18g

Desserts

33. German Pavilion Caramel Corn

Preparation time: 20 minutes

Cooking time: 25 minutes

Servings: 6

Ingredients:

- ½ cup popcorn kernels
- 2 cups of sugar
- 1 cup light corn syrup
- 1 ½ stick salted butter
- 1 can evaporate milk
- ¼ cup of coconut oil
- 1 teaspoon kosher salt

Directions:

1. Warm the coconut oil until melted over medium to high heat in a deep pot with a lid.

2. Once done, add 2 to 3 kernels of the popcorn into the hot pot. Once they begin to pop, scoop them out & dump in the leftover kernels.

3. Quickly shake the pot to disperse the kernels evenly. Cover the pot with a lid & immediately remove it from the heat.

4. Wait for half a minute, and then put the pot over the heat again. Once the kernels begin to pop vigorously, start shaking the pot until the popping stops or slows down.

5. Put the popcorn into a large bowl immediately.

6. Wipe the popcorn pot out and then add 1 stick of butter followed by evaporated milk, sugar, corn syrup, and kosher salt, giving the ingredients a good stir.

7. Boil the mixture over high heat.

8. Continue to stir the ingredients until the candy thermometer reflects 266 F, mixing the ingredients' entire time.

9. Remove, then stir in the additional stick of butter.

10. The moment it melts, immediately dump the popcorn into the pot & stir until nicely coated.

11. Put the popcorn onto a sheet pan and evenly spread it, then let completely cool, then break it into smaller bits. Serve and enjoy.

Nutrition:

Calories: 120

Carbs: 21g

Fat: 4g

Protein: 0g

34. Ginger Bread Popcorn

Preparation time: 20 minutes

Cooking time: 20 minutes

Servings: 4

Ingredients:

- ½ cup butter
- 1 bag Homestyle popcorn
- ¼ cup each of molasses & corn syrup
- 1 teaspoon vanilla
- ¾ cup packed brown sugar
- Wilton drizzle pouches; green and red
- ½ teaspoon each of:
- ground ginger
- cinnamon
- ground cloves
- baking soda
- ¼ teaspoon salt

Directions:

1. Preheat your oven to 250 F.

2. Pop the popcorn and pour them into a large-sized mixing bowl.

3. Prepare a large-sized cookie sheet with a silicone baking mat.

4. Then, over moderate heat in a large saucepan, heat the butter until melted, and add the molasses, ginger, corn syrup, brown sugar, ground cloves, cinnamon, and salt.

5. Boil the mixture within 3 to 5 minutes, stirring the ingredients now and then.

6. Remove the mixture from heat. Add the baking soda and vanilla.

7. Put the sauce on top of the popcorn immediately; toss to coat.

8. Spread the popcorn on the prepared cookie sheet & place them in the oven for an hour.

9. To prevent the popcorn from burning, don't forget to toss them every 15 minutes.

10. Let cool for an hour, and then drizzle the Wilton coating on top of the popcorn.

11. Gently break the popcorn & store them in an airtight container.

Nutrition:

Calories: 130

Carbs: 18g

Fat: 7g

Protein: 1g

35. Port Orleans Beignets

Preparation time: 35 minutes

Cooking time: 10 minutes

Servings: 20

Ingredients:

- 1-pound gluten-free pizza crust mix
- ½ cup plus 2 tablespoons apple juice
- 1 ½ teaspoon dry active yeast
- ¼ cup applesauce, unsweetened
- 2 ½ teaspoons powdered egg replacer, gluten-free
- ½ teaspoon canola oil
- A pinch of ground cinnamon
- ½ cup plus 2 tablespoons warm water
- 3 tablespoons sugar
- ¼ teaspoon salt
- Confectioners' sugar for finishing

Directions:

1. Combine the yeast with warm water in a small-sized mixing bowl, set aside for a couple of minutes.

2. Combine the apple juice with egg replacer, applesauce, oil, sugar, cinnamon & salt in the bowl of an electric mixer attached with a paddle attachment. Continue to mix until combined well.

3. Slowly add the pizza crust mix until soft dough forms. Put the dough onto a working surface lightly dusted with the leftover pizza crust mix.

4. Knead until the dough is no longer sticky but ensure that it's still soft.

5. Roll the dough out to approximately ¼" thickness & then cut into 2×3" pieces. Set aside for 20 minutes at room temperature.

6. Fill a deep-sided pot with approximately 2" of oil and heat it over medium heat.

7. Lightly press the beignets until slightly flatten. Add some of the beignets to the hot oil & fry until both sides turn golden brown, turning once or twice.

8. Using a slotted spoon, remove from the hot oil & place them on a paper towel-lined baking sheet. Just before serving, don't forget to dust with a generous amount of the confectioners' sugar.

Nutrition:

Calories: 71

Carbs: 9g

Fat: 4g

Protein: 1g

Conclusion

We hope it was informative and provided you with all of the tools you need to achieve your goals, making the most delicious 'take-out' in your kitchen. The next move is to collect all the necessary ingredients to make delicious meals and treats.

You will also need to understand and know how to store your masterpiece selections properly. For meals scheduled to be eaten at least three days after cooking, freezing is a great option. Freezing food is safe and convenient, but it doesn't work for every type of meal. You can also freeze the ingredients for a slow cooker meal and then dump out the container into the slow cooker and leave it there. It saves a lot of time and means you can pre-prep meals up to one to two months in advance.

You must also know and understand the proper ways to reheat your meals. Most people opt to microwave their meals for warming, but you can use any other conventional heating source in your kitchen as well. However, you have to be careful with microwaving because over-cooking can cause food to taste bad.

To combat this, cook your food in one-minute intervals and check on it between each minute. You can also help your food cook more evenly and quickly but keeping your meat cut into small pieces when you cook it. You should never put food directly from the freezer into the microwave. Let your frozen food thaw first when it's possible.

Food reheating and prep safety will become second nature over time. However, mistakes do happen, and as such, it's best to cook for short periods rather than longer ones, so you have less of a risk of making a mistake and needing to scrap everything you have prepared for that substantial amount of time. While it is a lot and seems complicated, meals prepping is the best way to set yourself up for success using your delicious copycat recipes. Make the meals using double the products and adjust the times; that is all it is to it!

Don't store hot food in the fridge. Keep your refrigerator at the proper temperature (should be below 40° Fahrenheit). If your refrigerator is warmer than this, it promotes the growth of bacteria. Any drastic temperature changes will cause condensation to form on the food items. You need to let your prepared food cool down in the open air - before placing it in a container, then closing the lid. The increased moisture levels can open the door to bacteria growth.

There are some other things you have to consider when freezing your meals. You should always label your container with the date that you put it in the freezer. You also need to double-check that your bottles, jars, or bags are each sealed tightly. If your containers aren't air-tight, your food will become freezer burnt and need to be trashed. We hope these additional suggestions will make your Copycat Recipes a treasured item in beside you.

Lastly, never stop yourself from the fear of mistakes or errors, as they are common. Enjoy cooking these meals as much as you enjoy having them. We, too, have given these recipes several trials only to master them. So better give it a try, and share it with others to inspire them all.

Why not get started right now? Have fun, and enjoy the time and money saved cooking at home!

CPSIA information can be obtained
at www.ICGtesting.com
Printed in the USA
BVHW091920230621
610293BV00007B/922